AIDS SHAMAN 2

Through the Veils

by Shokti

Cover drawing by Kairos

© **2019 Mark Whiting.**

Dedicated to Faerie Genie, Andy Saich, pioneer of queer conscious community

ONCE UPON A TIME

all the worlds lived together

there was no separation between matter and spirit

humans talked daily to the dead

to the trees, the plants, the animals

and remembered to honour the faerie elementals

who kept nature in balance

.

gradually humanity lost the connection

became obsessed with the material plane

but remembered the spirit as the Great Mother

holding, loving, feeding us all -

until the men of war rose to dominate the world

and set a Father God on her throne

dictating laws and condemning sinners

but still the people could recall

that spirit was real and that they had lived before

in other forms and would do so ever more...

.

It was the Roman Emperor, not the Church

who eradicated reincarnation from the Christian worldview

male priests seized the spiritual power that had long belonged
to the women, transgender and queer peoples,

male priests claimed to hold the keys to heaven:

instead of ecstatic rites that brought people in touch

with divine presence,

they went to church to hear the preacher

tell them God could only be known after death

and only if they obeyed the Church's rules in life...

All this served to create a frightened population

forced to be soldiers, workers, slaves and, nowadays
consumers

doing the bidding of their masters:

kept docile now by capitalism, media, alcohol and drugs

until we no longer even believe

in the transcendent possibilities of our souls....

until we have no sense of our ability to be whole

to be One with all creation

to rise daily to a natural elation

dancing with the spirit of Life

remembering the source of existence is Love.

But in these darker times
as Ignorance dominates the planet
millions of hearts are opening and souls remembering
this is not how it has to be:
the biggest threat to the military industrial complex
is the people remembering that I am another You
and You are another Me:
Seeing through the lies, all the way to infinity.

.

Everything we think we know will change -
we can live multidimensionally
enter the dance of synchronicity
unravel the knots and blocks in our souls
make the remembrance of ONENESS our greatest goal
restore again the holy Whole
each one of us has a role.

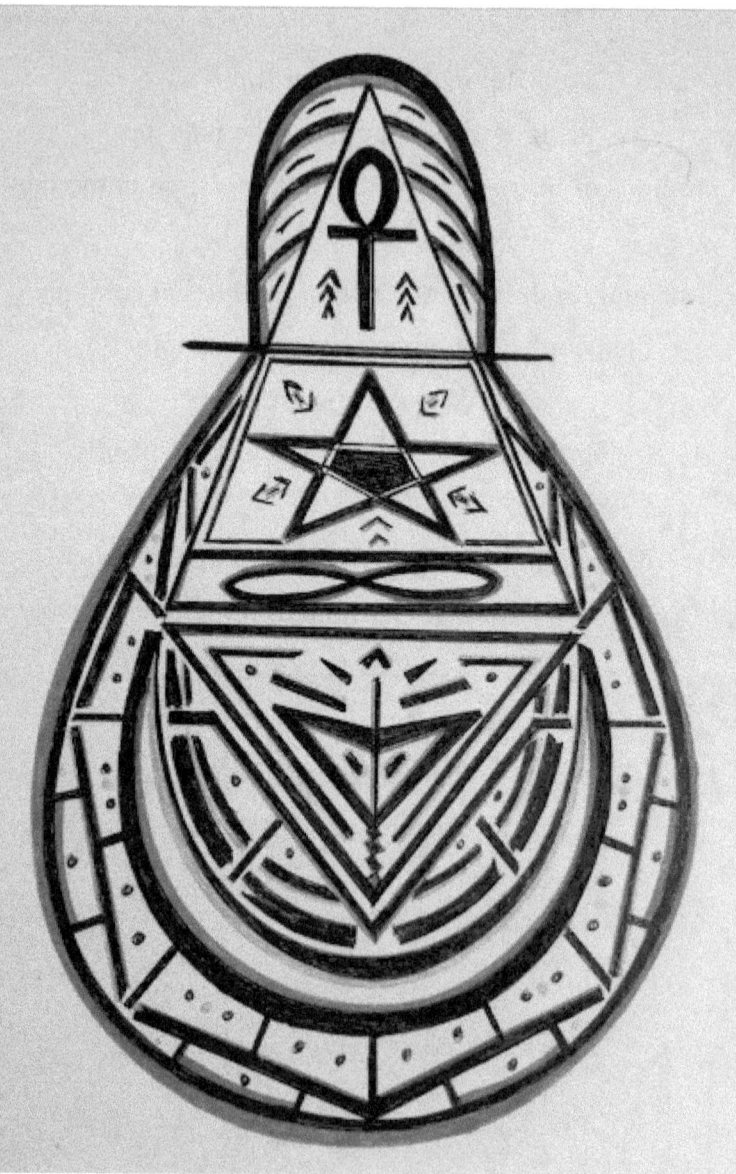

PART ONE

Accelerated Individual Discovery of Self

Transpersonal psychologist Dowling Singh wrote in the Advocate in December 1998 that Accelerated Individual Discovery of Self was the AIDS community's "secret understanding."

Writing of his experience as a hospice worker with dying men, Dowling said, –

"One of these men who I grew to love told me that, more than any other rite of passage in his life, through this harsh passage of AIDS he had come to know himself. He said he had always treated his life as though it were a dress rehearsal but that 'dying is very real.' It was, he said, through new eyes that he saw his own real beauty, his own real value, the depth of meaning we miss so often in life, and the raw power of love."

AIDS brought me an Accelerated Individual Discovery of Self/Soul/Spirit....

the fulfilment of a story in which we are soul entities, not one-lifetime body-minds, suddenly reaching the point where we are ready to **REMEMBER**

.... ready to **AWAKEN**

..... ready to **REALISE**.....

... ready to **SEE** that we have been here for a very long time indeed, that we have passed through the veils of life and death so many times. Souls reaching the point where we can know – while still in the body – that we have been travelling and searching and growing on this planet in order to come to this point of **RECALL** where - at the darkest hour - all would be revealed: we would see and learn to understand these soul journeys as we come to accept that our souls are immortal. In body after body we have lived and loved and learnt and lost. But now we might see there was a point to it all...

we took this journey to bring CONSCIOUSNESS into matter, so that we could live as enlightened, unencumbered, eternal and free beings IN PHYSICAL FORM.

And the key to this awakening is to see that the truth is right here in plain sight:

in the language of the Hindus, the Atman is Brahman, the individual self is the divine Self in all things

in the language of the Celtic Pagans we are Spirit, manifesting through earth, air, fire and water in the language of the Christian mystics, we are made in the image of God – male and female in the image of God, ie each one of us is both masculine and feminine, and as Jesus said in Gospel of Thomas, when we unite the male and female within, we can enter heaven

tantric practices, which engage sexual energies as holy and pathways to awakening, teach the same practice of uniting the male and female

and it was also taught in the Goddess temples of the ancient world for many millennia

where, as in pre-Christian cultures across the globe, the individuals who embodied both male and female spirit strongly in themselves, fulfilled the sacred roles

the sacred roles that connected the worlds

through rituals of music and ecstatic dance

sometimes achieved through sexual congress

in which the priest/ess would embody the deity

and make love to the seeker.

These sacred roles were taken away, so men might

control people's souls and make them OBEY:

our beautiful love so long denied and defiled

until the sorcery once associated with sodomy, sapphism and genderfluidity was completely forgotten

and reborn pagan witches, shamans and fools

could re-emerge in the world as the QUEER & the GAY

.... the mystery of why we're born this way...

Gay sex is witchcraft

The phallus is sacred
The anus is the gateway to paradise
The kingdom of heaven is found within

Sodomy and sorcery
Are ancient bedfellows
Sapphics once served Aphrodite,
Goddess of love and Artemis, of the hunt.
Transgendered holy souls
Served in the temples for millennia
Until the men of war
Adopting the sign of the sacrificed messiah
Sought to take control
Destroy the holy whole:

They sent the queers to the gutter
And kept the women in the bedroom
But the tide is turning
Homosex is out of the closet
Queer spirit on the rise
Time to expose the lies
Time to reclaim the body
Holy in all its parts
Time to reclaim queerness
As a magical art

I AWOKE TO LIFE THROUGH DEATH, WOKE UP TO SPIRITUALITY THROUGH SEXUALITY, DISCOVERED LOVE CAUSES US TO EVOLVE, REALISED IN ETERNITY WE NEVER GET OLD

and eternity exists at the core of our being

Physicists say it, mystics have always said it,

ravers take drugs to feel it –

EVERYTHING IS ENERGY

MOVING, CHANGING CONSTANTLY

WE HUMANS ARE ITS CHANNELS- CONDUITS

WE CREATE THE WORLD WE LIVE IN

WE HAVE NOT YET UNDERSTOOD HOW POWERFUL WE ARE

Like children we have enjoyed our toys, unaware for a long time that we were destroying the planet that enables us to live, using up its resources and wiping out many of its inhabitants. Like madmen we have developed technologies that we can use to destroy ourselves

NOT REALISING WE ARE ALL ONE, WE COMPETE, WE FIGHT, WE DESTROY

Ignoring the strongest impulse in us –

TO LIVE IN PEACE, TO LOVE, TO CELEBRATE

How many on earth now want to continue to live the old dramas of conflict? The earth is in crisis. Time is running out

Voices of peace and compassion must become stronger than those of conflict and hate

OR IT MAY BE TOO LATE

"We are arriving at one of the most fruitful and important turning points in the history of the race. the Self is entering into relation with the Body. for, that the individual should conceive and know himself, not a toy and a chance-product of his own bodily heredity, but as identified and continuous with the Eternal Self of which his body is a manifestation, is indeed to begin a new life and to enter a hitherto undreamed world of possibilities....this transformation, whilst the greatest and most wonderful, is also of course the most difficult in Man's evolution, for him to effect. it may roughly be said that the whole of the civilisation-period in Man's history is the preparation for it."

EDWARD CARPENTER

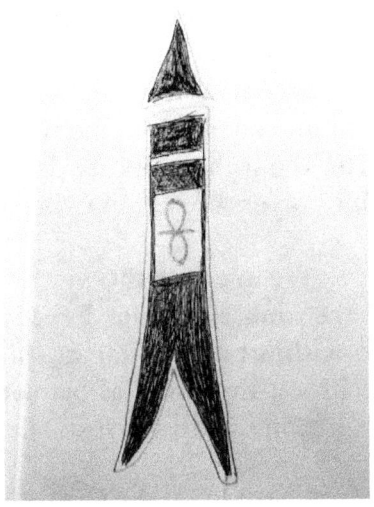

In some parts of the world there are more men exploring their sexual desires for other men more freely, more frequently than ever before.
In others men like us live in fear as do other queers.
AIDS taught us that unbridled sexuality is dangerous.
Drug addiction and dark abusive sexual scenarios are teaching the same thing now to many men.

But sexuality is divine, is holy
It can transform us, uplift us or destroy us
We play with fire when we connect sexually with others
Even more so when we take chemicals too
We shift our consciousness through an act of will
Which is the definition of magic
We are witch souls, shamans, playing our games as we always did
But now there are so many of us
And we have so little idea what we are doing.

Fire is the element that lifts us to Spirit
That sets our souls alight
When we play we are praying
Pumping energy into the world
But if our thoughts are dark
Our prayers come out twisted.

We are called Gay
Because we are souls ready for Freedom and Joy
But without an anchor in spirit
Without the spirit of prayer
A man can get lost.

If we look for, recognise and give love to god in each other
when we meet
Our prayerful play will open heaven's gates
It will be better than Tina, than Mephedrone, than G
It will be the triumphant return of Sodomy
To the Holy Act it was designed to be.

When Bodies and Souls unite
We give birth to Light.

Sapphism, Sodomy and Sorcery are ancient bedfellows.

*"At the time of the birth of Christ, cults of men devoted to a
Goddess flourished throughout the broad region extending
from the Mediterranean to south Asia. While galli were
missionizing the Roman Empire, kalu, kurgarru and assinnu
continued to carry out ancient rites in the temples of
Mesopotamia, and the third gender predecessors of the hijra
were clearly evident in India. To complete the picture we
should also mention the eunuch priests of Artemis at Ephesus;
the western Semitic qedeshim, the male "temple prostitutes"
known from the Hebrew Bible and Ugartici texts of the late
second millennium; and the keleb, priests of Astarte at Kition
and elsewhere. Beyond India, modern ethnographic literature
documents gender variant shaman-priests throughout southeast
Asia, Borneo and Sulawesi. All these roles share the traits of
devotion to a goddess, gender transgression and
homosexuality, ecstatic ritual techniques and actual (or
symbolic) castration."*

From 'Priests of the Goddess: Gender Transgression in Ancient Religion' by
WILL ROSCOE

HIV CAME TO US TO BE
THE END OF DISEASE
A GATEWAY TO ETERNITY
this is my message and I will say it over and over
THERE IS NO DEATH
THERE IS NO SEPARATION
the time has come to break down the old paradigms
and defeat the darkness that grips the world
the time has come to birth a new humanity
that puts love, cooperation and peace at the centre of the play
the world is gripped by darkness and fear
but the solution to all our woes has always been here
in our hearts.

PART TWO

Queers On The Turn

"Gay people are bellwethers, early adopters, leading indicators; as well the "canaries-in-the-mine," poised on the cutting (bleeding?) edge of evolution. Whether we know it or not—or call ourselves gay or not—our lives and struggles change the world. And there's still more changing to do."

TOBY JOHNSON

Canaries in the Meth Mine

The second sexual revolution has been building since the turn
of the millennium
once AIDS had disappeared from our hospitals and gay bars.

Dating websites were the start of the cyber game, which gay
men embraced with gusto,
where drug deals and dates started to become a normal
combination in some quarters.

Gaydar – gay romeo dominated
Recon held the fetish market
moving to the darker zones of bbrts – bareback realtime sex
and nastykinkpigs where the doings got deviant and dirty.

Meth was a rarity at first
but the examples of Sydney and the USA could have shown us
in London,
that meth is a manifest curse.

The smoking ban in clubs had an effect,
dance floor flow was disrupted:
outdoor smoking changed the night out,
many guys started to prefer to party at home
where they could also consume sacraments in peace.

Grindr, Scruff, Tindr and the ilk
suddenly made partying from home so much more fun -
dates could be arranged and deals could be done;
shopping for sex, for satisfaction
for adventure or distraction
bodies on the screen
for free or for sale
no love involved,

so drugs are what we need
to free the mind, feel the high and find the connection -
but there are sacrifices that can follow
like a fucked mind and no erection.
An addiction quickly acquired that makes no sense,
sex sacrificed to a game of pretence.

.

20 years ago very few gay men injected drugs,
in the second decade of the 21st century 'slamming' has
become common.
No need to repeat the horror stories here -
gay men are not listening to them anyway.
Meth high continues to draw men in to the tinaverse,
perhaps meth is a manifest curse.

Canaries in the meth mine,
in the consumer age
use me, use you, take me, feed you
men use each other like commodities
and sex becomes a selfish fulfilling of need, a seeking of seed
to temporarily fulfil a deeply felt need:
**a gay man ultimately seeks to feel and know the god inside
him through the love of another man.**

.

Canaries in the meth MIND:
men forget how to love, how to make love without the chem,
lose empathy and the ability to care about others
as their own inner unacknowledged pain becomes immense.
this manifest curse is a reversal of our humanity
it makes no sense
- but is this the future for the human race?
slaves to the machine, manifest in our hands
everyone an object to be utilised at will

the deadly threat of aids kept at bay by a pill:
canaries in the meth mine.

Obsessed with economics, politics and war
in the post AIDS era
humanity is walking blindly through the open door
of liberated sexual behaviour.
We need to talk about the second sexual revolution.
understand the Pandora's box we've opened:
the canaries in the meth mine
are dying because sexuality is still not understood

A man's body is a miracle
his love is a gateway to heaven:
as loving brothers gay men could be changing the world
welcoming young men into a healthy, respectful, conscious
scene -
we need to face our demons to free our minds and hearts
meet each man with love if we wish our sexual activities to
nourish our souls
the shame was imposed on us, the guilt and the fear
it's time we shook off these wounds
that led us into Aids and lead into addiction
for we have the power to create a world built on love of
man for man
creating in Oneness with women and trans:
It's a simple and divine plan.

The manifest curse is decimating us
as the manifest disease did before,
but healing comes when we embrace every aspect of life as
divine play and drop the constant craving for more.

The healing comes when we find queer family, queer friends
with whom our heart aligns and we share the best times.
The healing comes when we remember love
is what drove us to come out in the first place

The healing comes when we remember we are Spirit
here to live out a dream:
we weren't born for suffering,
we are GAY, we are lovers of life Herself
but we need to urgently attend to our own spiritual,
emotional and mental health

In 50 years since Stonewall we have manifested a global
revolution,
but our community contains suffering, abuse and pain:
as we are celebrating our massive achievements
we must seek to change the narrative told in the world, the
narrative about who we are
no longer the outcasts, the perverted, the sick

we are the wounded healers, we are artists and seekers:
it's time for us to truly claim our worth
and see an end to the manifest curse.

Canaries in the meth mind:
scouts on the extreme edge of the second sexual revolution.
All of us
need to remember
a gay man ultimately seeks to feel and know the god inside
him through the love of another man

"The position that gay people take in society, the function we so often choose, is that of mediator between worlds..... In a tribal environment, this means shape shifting into wolves, birds, stones, wind and translating their wisdoms for the benefit of the people of the tribe... in the long patriarchal history that has gradually enveloped the world's people, the gay function has been to make crossover journeys between gender-worlds, translating, identifying and bringing back the information ....gay culture is always on the cusp of each intersecting world or way of life, on the path between one world and another."

JUDITH GRAHN

Something every queer should know...

"There is a pervasive association at all times in the ancient world between eunuchs, women and religion... In the Bible, this linkage is reflected in the mentions of "the holy ones," who, in addition to being called holy, are also called "sodomites" and "whores" in the King James translation and "temple prostitutes" in recent versions. The demand for celibacy of the clergy under the Roman Catholic system reflects the same association. People expect their priests to have no children because childless gay men and lesbians were the original chaste, holy priests. Moreover, gay people mirror in themselves the divine union of maleness and femaleness that is traditionally thought to be the image of the Creator. After all, the image of the Creator is male and female, according to Genesis 1:28.

"Straight people, who suffer from a gender imbalance, marry one another in order to bring the male and female sides together. But gay people are closer to having both sides in balance within themselves. Transgendered and intersexed persons are even closer to that holy state."

Historian RICTOR NORTON

MAY THE SPIRIT RETURN TO THE PEOPLE

From whom She was ripped apart

May the Spirit return to the people

– As the Queer Healers remember their Art.

The Warrior swords of the Crucified Christ from the 4th century onwards closed down our temples and slaughtered the trans priestesses, women witches, genderfluid shamans and male sodomites, a persecution lasting over 1000 years, intensifying from the the 11th century.
The political state took over this persecution from the 16th century - the death penalty was in place for sodomy in the UK until 1861.

But the climate of fear, of arrests and blackmail hit another peak for gay men in the 20th century

And while the change over the past 50 years since Stonewall has been incredible –

No wonder we are a segment of humanity with health issues

Of course we are a people with emotional baggage that needs to be addressed

the issues arising from both HIV and CHEMSEX are the clear symptom of this wound

**THE HISTORICAL PERSECUTION OF QUEER PEOPLE NEEDS TO BE UNDERSTOOD AND ADDRESSED.
OUR QUEER SPIRIT – REPRESSED FOR SO LONG – NEEDS ROOM TO BREATHE, ROOM TO HEAL, ROOM TO BECOME WHAT IT TRULY IS**

—   Still in the world today so many of our queerkind still
     have to live secret lives
     have to live with fear, and the danger of arrest,
     violence, death

     the roots of homophobia, transphobia and biphobia are
patriarchal and religious, they are about power and domination

     across the world, our Gay Liberation is linked to the
liberation of the whole of humanity, to our evolution as a
species, into wisdom, into multidimensionality, into LOVE

                    **we are the healers, we are called
                                this is our time**

—   **TIME TO CHANGE THE STORY ABOUT WHO
     WE ARE – NO LONGER THE SICK OR
     SINNING, WE ARE THE WOUNDED HEALERS,
     THE SCOUTS AND SHAMANS, MEDIATORS,
     PEACE-BRINGERS, CONNECTORS OF
     WORLDS, MEDIATORS FOR THE DYING.**

"If anything is sacred, the human body is sacred"
WALT WHITMAN

"Our beautiful lovely sexuality is the gateway to spirit. Under all organised religions of the past, Judaism, Christianity, Islam, there has been a separation of carnality, or shall we say of flesh or earth or sex, and spirituality. As far as I am concerned they are all the same thing, and what we need to do as faeries is to tie it all back together again."
HARRY HAY

—

**LGBTIQ+ liberation TODAY is intrinsically linked
to the decrease in religious control over society**

Yet our ultimate liberation is intimately linked to the
**SPIRITUAL AWAKENING OF THE WHOLE OF
HUMANITY**
as religion is replaced … not by a soulless materialism (we
can already see that is destroying people and planet) but
by a **HIGHER UNDERSTANDING**
**an AQUARIAN outlook on the multidimensional nature
of existence**

Part of that understanding, coming through our many
lettered diverse community is that the HUMAN SOUL
IS NOT LIMITED BY GENDER, SEXUALITY OR
ANY OTHER DIVIDING LINE THAT HUMAN
MINDS GET SO EXCITED ABOUT

**THE BREAKDOWN OF LONG HELD
CONVENTIONS AND TABOOS AROUND
SEXUALITY AND GENDER IS A SIGN THAT
THE SPECIES IS READY FOR THE NEXT
STAGE OF OUR EVOLUTION**

**where we remember we are not form
we are not thought
we are not emotion
WE ARE SPIRIT
eternal and free
and the doorway to self-knowledge
to oneness with All
is
LOVE**

MARRIED TO LOVE, MARRIED TO PAN
MEETING HIM IN EVERY MAN
EXPLORING AN ANCIENT WAY FOR TODAY
FINDING THE DIVINITY IN EVERY CONNECTION
CUM WHAT MAY

CALL OF NATURE, CALL OF THE GODDESS
TO THE SONS OF THE UNIVERSE
A DIVINE INHERITANCE AWAITS THE SOULS
OF THE AWAKENING CHILDREN OF PLANET EARTH

EROS, PAN, HERNE, CERNUNNOS
SEX IS THE KEY, TAKE IT DOWN OFF THE CROSS
BROTHERHOODS EXPRESSING UNITY
IN EROTIC, EXOTIC, ECSTATIC COMMUNITY

THE GREAT MOTHER RETURNS
HER HORNED SON CUM HOME
FLESH UNITED WITH SOUL AND SPIRIT
WE REMEMBER CONNECTION
IT WAS ALWAYS THERE
BUT FORGOTTEN IN THE MADNESS
OF A WORLD THAT DOESN'T CARE

AWAKENING THE HEARTS OF MEN
TO THE MIRACLE THAT LIVES IN THEM
TO THE POWER IN SEX AND IN THE SOUL
TO THE GLORY OF BECOMING WHOLE

THE WOMEN ARE WAITING
THEIR HEARTS ARE ALREADY OPEN
AND GENDER RULES ARE BREAKING
IDENTITY'S TOWER IS SHAKING
MEN BECOMING WHOLE IS THE GOAL

MEN CAUSE ALL WARS
MEN LEAD CORPORATE CORRUPTION
MEN DOMINATE IN GOVERNMENT
MEN DRILL FOR OIL
MEN KILL MEN, AND WOMEN AND CHILDREN TOO
MEN NEED TO GROW UP
AND LEARN SOMETHING NEW

ECSTATIC BROTHERS, LIBERATED SISTERS
BEINGS OF ALL GENDERS AND NONE
THE AGE OF AQUARIUS - WHERE WE GROW INTO
THE LIGHT OF THE SOUL -

HAS BEGUN...

WE ENTER THROUGH HONOURING
THE FEMININE
THE HALF THAT HAS BEEN DOWNTRODDEN
THE GODDESS IN EVERY MAN AND WOMAN
THE MOTHER MIND THAT REVEALS LOVE
AS THE CREATIVE, UNITING FORCE
TIME TO BRING HUMANITY
BACK ON COURSE

"The 21st century paradigm shift from an old gay assimilation/sexual orientation model to a new gay essentialism/societal contribution model is similar in meaning to the 20th century paradigm shift from Newtonian to Einsteinian physics, a scientific and social revolution causing a radical, fundamental change in how gay people perceive reality, role and identity. It illuminates the unique and essential way in which gay people see and move in the world, select careers and social roles, and contribute to society for the benefit of all beings"

— Radical Faerie founding father and queer elder
DON KILHEFNER

I USED TO GO DRINKING IN BARS

used to go cruising in parks,
but nowadays i can sit home alone
and 'cruise for love' on a mobile phone

I used to watch men wanking in cottages,
now i sit at home and watch them wanking on web cams.
i used to enjoy fucking bareback,
with other positive brothers on meds
but now that everyone wants it raw
I'll often use a condom instead.

I used to enjoy a chem sacrament,
to deepen the sex-love-spirit connection -
but for some reason now guys take drugs
that destroy all chance of them getting an erection,
they take the drug then seek the sex
sitting home alone on their mobile phones....
but finding a lover then taking the trip...
is what really gets us in the zone.

The gay boys all rush to the city,
the gay boys so easily get lost:
I talk to guys who have done every sex act, every drug,
been adored and explored to the max,
been raped and used, been desperate to be abused,
but they've never wandered the parks
and met a man in the trees,
they've never fucked just on beautiful, quality weed:
they've dived in the deep end
found excess, been high and of course been depressed
so hard to see the way out of the viper's nest.

It used to be you had to work quite hard to be a slut,
risk attack or arrest in parks and toilets -
even the saunas got raided in the 1980s.
Sex is plentiful in the internet age,
masc seeking masc is all the rage:
the toilets are closed but now we cruise on the phone:
a backroom in every bedroom.

The chains are breaking on the homosexual cage
but there's more to discover about our sexuality
as we enter the Aquarian Age.

These days we meet to play, we rarely mention love,
but guys:
what we need is friends,
the chance to make amends
and find some innocence again,
see where love can take us
but don't expect affairs to last forever:
every lover is a precious gift, a holy joy
and when we know how to open our hearts
sexuality itself gets us high

There's one way the sex scene is SOOOO much better today:
we have safe, legal clubs where we can go to play,
where men meet men for a pint and a cruise,
wander through darkrooms, dance together, get naked:
all this without the fear of the law,
this is much much better than it was before.
Social sexual spaces can bond our brotherhood
Ecstatic behaviours feed our souls......

If we let our play be divine
we bring our souls online.
Through love for each brother
we can liberate one another

Sex can open the gates to heaven,
the multidimensional Self:
that's part of what gay sex is actually for
in the grand scheme of creation -
it's what we were honoured for
in pagan temples around the world,
the phallus was the symbol of God,
the body was holy in the age of the Goddess -
the temple of the spirit divine

and the task in the 21st century
is to renew this understanding for this time

The religions of the Father forbade our passion,
made the body taboo and sex a sin:
to control the minds and souls of the people:
the queers have always known by instinct
that sex can liberate the soul,
maybe we knew this more than anyone else:
and in all our searching, our highs and lows
we are seeking to regain this knowledge again.

It's why gay sex is now soooo much in fashion,
for the old ways are rising again:
the human spirit seeks freedom from its chains,
the Aquarian light of liberation is shining on Piscean pain.
Some will fear annihilation
and some will see

we're in an acceleration of frequencies
that is not just affecting the climate:
the collective human soul is bursting to give birth
to light filled rainbow consciousness,
where all are seen for their worth
and the magic ones return....

Gatekeepers, Witches, Shamans and Fools:
Time to reunite Sapphism and Sodomy with Sorcery
Gender-variance with the Gods of Old

Time to redefine ourselves
not by how we fuck
but by hearts and minds
by the gifts of spirit we bring for the whole

we need to find our sanctuaries, our groves and our tribes
to reclaim our gifts and strengthen our souls
so that the healing of our planet home can begin
and the healing of the collective human whole
a process in which sexuality
so long denied, despised and analysed
plays a crucial, sacred role.

PART THREE

Into Oneness

"If I go into the place in myself that is love, and you go into the place in yourself that is love, we are together in love. Then you and I are truly in love, the state of being love. That's the entrance to Oneness."

RAM DASS

THE MOTHER MIND

There's two halves to the brain and two halves to the mind:
the individualised self and the collective self, through which we
can know our interconnection, our oneness with all things,
but we live in a world that is only honouring the individual
consciousness

In the world today we are trained to be Warriors
to approach life as a competition, a battle, a war to be won
But inside each of us also is the Universal Mother Mind
which is easy to access just by being kind
and loving to the whole wide world
just like She would be
through Her in Us we feel, intuit, know and experience
inter-dependence, universal love and liberty
we know we are eternal, we know we are free.

We glimpse her on the dance floor, on weed
on acid, mushrooms and ayahuasca
but if we embrace the Mother within us all
and take care of the planet and each other
the transformation of humanity will come faster

CONSCIOUSNESS is a thing...

A thing we all have in common:

it can be charted, mapped and explored.

Just as there is a physical universe,

there are also vast mental, emotional and spiritual layers of
creation -

each one as vast as the physical, as complex,

each one open to our searching.

CONSCIOUSNESS is a magical thing

it operates through attraction, love and karma:

it is opened through compassion, selflessness, service

through devotion and knowledge.

Our beliefs shape our reality,

we open or close our own gates:

it's our choice to explore or ignore

the potential of the cosmic human,

birthing a multidimensional age

that was long foreseen

in so many prophecies

and so many dreams.

There are many

MAPS OF CONSCIOUSNESS

in existence, such as the chakra system, the kabbalistic tree of life and the astrological wheel of the year. We can ignore, deny these things, but that basically leaves us as pawns of life, destined to suffer the swings and dives until we perhaps find a route to wisdom. If we study the wisdom traditions whose roots pre-date religions, and which survive despite the prevailing scientific rational outlook, we can become pioneer psychonauts unlocking the secrets of the mystery of consciousness we all find ourselves in.

A simple way of describing what we come to do here on planet Earth: to find, then to love, express and be – ourselves. Each one of us a unique version of the One Consciousness. But to love ourselves means to love all of Creation.

THE UNIVERSE IS A LOVE STORY

a tale of sex and passion:

from the atom to the human

everything in creation seeks connection

and that's why for countless centuries

the holiest of symbols were the cunt and the erection

.

Cut off by religion from the sacred in sexuality,

from the holiness of the flesh:

denied the generous polyamorous potential of love

we've been cut off from the source within,

from the eternal dance of the lover and beloved,

we've been *deluded* by the concept of sin

.

To tune into the romantic dance of the subtle planes

we need to be aware that we exist in a divine game,

to attune the body and the mind

to be free of guilt and shame about sex -

for the way to the infinite source of love

is to marry the female and male on the INSIDE -

to release the primal self

to be a raw passionate lover of life is the source of health:

the source of true inner wealth.

CONSCIOUSNESS is the mystery
and planet earth is the school
we'll never discover what it's all about
by denying the seekers and teachers who came before
nor will we awaken to wisdom
by obeying all the rules
for rules are designed to constrain us
and divide the world into wrong and right
cutting us off from the source of Light

Reality is a rainbow miracle
and humanity is on the verge
of a breakthrough, a revelation
a cosmic Aquarian surge.
The Sun, the Moon, the stars, the planets
The Earth herself are with us on the Way
Consciousness is the miracle
and the solar system is the scene of the play
the game of awakening is ON

We are a UNITY experiencing DIVERSITY
a ONE become MANY
becoming ONE again.

Love, Light and Laughter

Play, Joy, Pleasure and Touch -

These are the divine gifts of the body

- seek out what makes the heart sing

when the shockwaves get too much

.

Many are losing it, but many are choosing

to become more aware, to care

Community of Souls is coming to Planet Earth.

Humanity's Aquarian Rebirth.

As psychedelic mystic Alan Watts said back in the 1960s....

"What you are basically, deep, deep down, far, far in, is simply the fabric and structure of existence itself. So, say in Hindu mythology, they say that the world is the drama of God. God is not something in Hindu mythology with a white beard that sits on a throne, that has royal prerogatives. God in Indian mythology is the self, Satchitananda. Which means sat, that which is, chit, that which is consciousness; that which is ananda is bliss. In other words, what exists, reality itself is gorgeous, it is the fullness of total joy."

"Who is it that loves and who that suffers? He alone stages a play with Himself; who exists save Him? The individual suffers because he perceives duality. It is duality which causes all sorrow and grief. Find the One everywhere and in everything and there will be an end to pain and suffering."

ANANDAMAYI MA

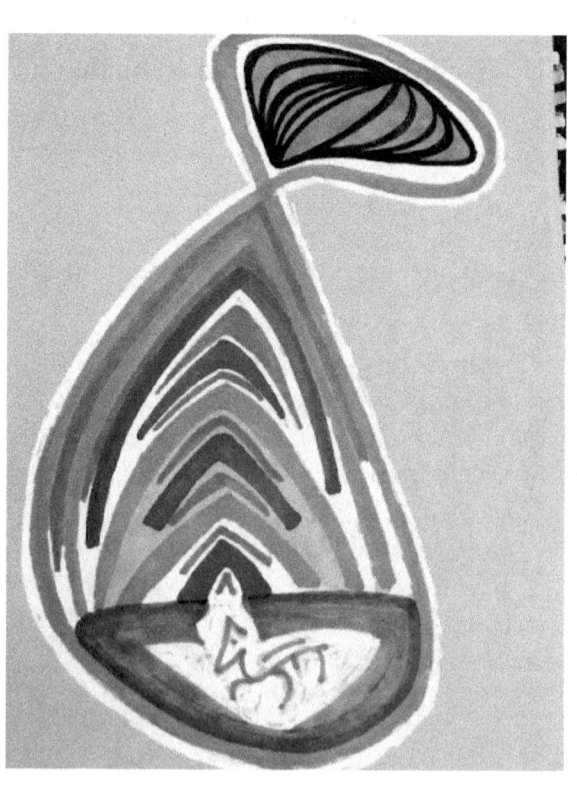

LOVE IS A GAME OF MIRRORS

I look, I feel, I see: another version of me.

We are all searching for the mirrors

that show us Who We Are,

looking for the hearts and hands

that open the soul and make us more whole

We are told that God is Love

and how delightfully simple that is....

Love is after all not a person, but a presence

within us and within all things

seeking to connect and grow:

in the game of mirrors we walk in the presence,

in the game of mirrors we drop the pretence

that love can ever be limited

Love reflected back one on one

has literally nowhere to go

that's why our mirrors creak, break, shatter

love is an expanding force, it's divine, it's not yours nor mine

if it's not expanding, moving, creating it will explode or fade in
time

In the game of mirrors
love reflects to infinity
and at the infinite speed of love
all boundaries disappear
so does all fear
we remember why we are here
and that's why all life seeks
to play the Game of Mirrors

Lovers often seek 'the one'
but misunderstand the search completely
it's not 'the' one to complete us that we need
it's 'The One' who lives in everybody

In the game of mirrors
THE One is looking for their way home
but our egos deceive us
and so we end up ALONE
but when the ego is surrendered
and love allowed to expand
in the game of mirrors
we can become ALL ONE

YOU ARE ANOTHER ME
I AM ANOTHER YOU
WITH THE LOVE IN OUR SOULS
WE CAN FIND OUR WAY THROUGH:
THE GAME OF MIRRORS
IS THE WAY HOME

"If you don't fill your days with love, you are wasting your life."
JAMES BROUGHTON

"Keep love in your heart. A life without it is like a sunless garden when the flowers are dead. The consciousness of loving and being loved brings a warmth and a richness to life that nothing else can bring."
OSCAR WILDE

"Someday, after mastering the winds, the waves, the tides and gravity, we shall harness for God the energies of love, and then, for a second time in the history of the world, man will have discovered fire."
PIERRE TEILHARD DE CHARDIN

"In ancient times, everyone knew that the love two people shared was not shared for themselves alone, but for and with the entire community. Shared love became a conduit for higher energies entering the physical plane. Sometimes this was seen as a sacred marriage, be it between a man and a woman, two women or two men. Through their union, two were known to be able to draw in archetypal energy, to anchor it in form. The archetypal patterns of A Man and A Woman Together, Two Women Together, and Two Men Together were laid down in the collective unconscious long before there was a sense of goddesses and gods, in the time before the ice, when people still encountered Oneness directly. To be whole, a culture needs to cultivate each of the three primary love patterns, for each carries a different energy. Two women together create a storage vessel for the collective. Two men together broadcast out that information to the collective. A man and a woman together celebrate the doorway to embodiment through their being together. As we journey into the future, we must also spiral back to the foundations of human consciousness to find our roots, so that we can build on them anew. The patterns in the collective unconscious are like mountain ranges, changing slowly, that define for us the horizon against which we see Eternity."

From **Two Flutes Playing** by ANDREW RAMER

"Don't look for a lover; BE ONE."

JAMES BROUGHTON

SEVEN WAVES OF BLISS

The first Bliss came in the late 1960s, the hippy revolution, the summer of love, the festivals

The second Bliss came in the late 1980s, house music, acid, the second summer of love

The third was in the mid 1990s, rave culture and pre-millennial ascension

The fourth in the early 2000s, the new age seemed not so far away

The fifth Bliss has been building since 2012, more gradually than those that went before and is with us now

Some are riding the wave, some are falling into the deep waters

Bliss is what's hitting us, though we may consider it crisis

Vibrational shift on personal and collective levels

body, mind, emotion, spirit: humanity waking up to Oneness

The sixth wave is coming in from 2020

and the seventh in the 2030s

It maybe takes 4 generations to shift the human spirit to a new way of being

70 years of struggle and strain, the battle between bliss and pain

between transcendence and destruction

With each wave of bliss the spirit world merges with the
physical

rebuilding the SACRED HOOP

the love consciousness field that unifies matter and spirit

a field held in place by human shamanic souls

from whom the power was taken long ago

and instead stored in cathedrals and churches

When the shamans held the sacred hoop in place

the people lived in the dance and presence of spirit at all times

there was little need for holy days or holy places

this was the Dreamtime, the Happy Hunting Ground, Arcadia

Our own shamanic past wiped out centuries ago, in the west

contacts with spirit still happen through mediums and mystics

but their offerings are ridiculed and diminished by society

which has been sold a consumerist dream of never ending
greed

and kept in a deep, deep sleep

When a wave of bliss hits

some wake up from the dream but then maybe

will fall again into confusion and pain:

to truly escape the mass delusion

we have to face many challenges on the way

and the best advice I ever got

was that when the going gets tough

the tough PRAY

.

With mind set on the goal, and ego the servant to the Whole

With heart open and compassion our greatest tool

We discover the Earth is one big Mystery School

.

On this journey we need allies, comrades, friends

For there may be a way to go yet

Until the dark age of division and confusion ends.

FREEDOM OF THE SPIRIT
Freedom of the Soul
FREEDOM OF THE BODY
and from any gendered roles
FREEDOM TO LOVE
and find out just Who We Are
FAGGOTS DYKES AND QUEERS
re-unite the earth and stars
we're coming out of the bars
to proclaim Who We Are
What we are, Why we are HERE
We gonna find out just WHY
we are here to be COSMIC AND QUEER.

We are all everyone and everything, change the perception change the experience.

Spirituality is engagement with the potential within us to evolve consciously into mindful, compassionate, passionate and peaceful warriors of the human species. It embraces the possibility that consciousness is not limited to our individual experiences, but is actually a collective experience which we are each one intrinsic part, equal to all others parts. Spirituality encourages us to develop respect for all living beings, for the planet and for the potential inherent in consciousness, which becomes accessible to us once the tiger within, the ego, is tamed and directed towards service to the planet and others.

There are hundreds of thousands of rainbow spirits incarnate on the planet at the moment who instinctively see through the lies and illusions being spread by governments, media, big business, military and financial interests who are profiting from the devastating destruction of the planet and its animals and from the division and discord between nations and faiths. Rainbow spirits see through the confusion spread by the battle between religions, and between religion and so-called 'scientific reason'. They are in touch with a higher truth, a greater perspective. Something happens in the life of a rainbow spirit that opens up the mind to the cosmos, and the heart to life.
We are everywhere. In every nation. In every generation. We see a truth beyond right and wrong, beyond conflict and greed, we embody soul essence that is beyond gender definitions, that cannot be limited by labels of sexuality Worldly power rarely interests us. But wherever we are we wield influence, we shine light, we bring love, we share joy.

.

"The sharing of joy, whether physical, emotional, psychic or intellectual, forms a bridge between the sharers which can be the basis for understanding much of what is not shared between them, and lessens the threat of their difference."

AUDRE LORDE

LOVE IS LOVE IS LOVE IS LOVE

whoever loves whomever
whether we love one or a lot
let's celebrate what we were born to do
let's celebrate our love
let's go beyond the lies and fear
embrace the love that is sacred and queer

love illuminates the dark
and opens up the skies
the power is in us to push the limits
and love all that is alive

the power is in you, in me
to create, to heal, community
let's go beyond what's been known before
live out the dream we came here for

love is love is love is love

holy however you look at it

SHIVA. DIONYSUS. ATHENA. PAN. KALI. ARTEMIS. DIANA. ISHTAR. CYBELE

The Ancient Ones call to us still

Life is not the random accident of biology

You are Myth and Story, Magic and History

the result of all that has gone before

and we all know this at our core

LOVE IS THE LAW

and while our bodies are matter, our souls are spirit:

WE ARE STARLIGHT AS WELL AS STARDUST

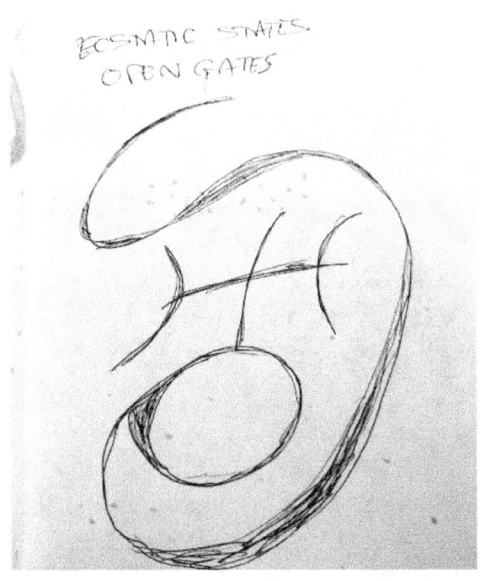

To escape from the insanity

that's deluding humanity –
embrace non-duality:
and go to the trees
sit in the breeze
absorb the fire
go to the rivers and seas

the western world got obsessed
with the notion of right and wrong
with the tragedy of darkness and light
became blind to the powers of second sight

but the eastern world saw
that there is really more
going on than these notions in the mind
the eastern world saw
that the world is a divine dream
and nothing is ever as black and white as it seems

inside the yang there is the yin
and the yin inside the yang
inside the female there is the male
inside the male the female
life is a myriad of possibilities
and every one will be explored
because as well as male and female, there is so much more

so it's really high time
in the 21st century
that the world listened and learned
and voices of bigotry, hate and separation
were finally and utterly IGNORED

.

WHERE ARE THE VOICES OF UNITY IN THE WORLD?

They are there but can they be heard
above the clamour of disarray and division?
Humanity on the brink
needs to come to a big decision

.

We have been lied to for long enough:
We're not born to serve the capitalist machine
we are born to live out our dreams
to love and grow and enjoy life
find our own part in the divine dream

.

BECAUSE IT'S TIME TO WAKE UP
and those in deep sleep will suffer
but those who truly LOVE
and practise COMPASSION
will find another
WAY
we approach the holiest of days
when humanity finally is AWAKE.

The men of war made sex taboo

held down the power of women
made the queers feel shame
that's how they took control
cut us all off from the whole:
without a strong feminine
and the queers with no role
the magic of life was lost
the earth, once our mother, became a resource
we are now seeing on the planet
the tragic cost:
mass extinction, all life under threat
the biggest step in humanity's evolution
the biggest challenge yet.

Only by shifting our understanding of life
can humanity hope to change its ways and survive:
the good news on this terrifying journey is....
the Goddess and her Servants
are still right here, alive...

RECLAIM the magic ...

...of spiritualised same sex love

RECLAIM the magic...

...of sacred transsexuality

RECLAIM the magic of the drumbeat
of communal ecstatic dance
of bliss beyond boundaries of individuality

RECLAIM the magic of open hearts and minds
of being gentle, being kind
RECLAIM the magic of the body as a temple of the soul
of the journey, the quest to be whole

RECLAIM the magic of the fire circle
of water as a purifier
of fresh air and free thinking
of the earth as sacred

RECLAIM the magic
of the seasons, the moon and the stars
RECLAIM magic
of genderfluidity, gendervariance, genderfuckery
RECLAIM the magic
of women's radical power and spirit
RECLAIM the magic
of sacred brotherhood between men who love men

RECLAIM THE MAGIC
of Presence
of Great Spirit
the Great Mother

RECLAIM THE MAGIC
of Her queer priest/priestesses
of Dionysian rites
Pan worship and sacred ceremony
in nature
with an army of lovers

RECLAIM THE MAGIC
of the inner child
of inner marriage
of sexuality as a divine gift that reveals the soul
of the mystery of existence

RECLAIM THE MAGIC
of breaking away from the stifling norm
of being alive in human form

RECLAIM THE MAGIC OF NATURE
as the spring rises may we rise too
out of deep slumber into the wonder of the soul
as the summer comes may we shine like the sun
and play like the lion
as the autumn falls may we turn within with grace
as the winter lands may we heal in sacred space

the dance of spirit on the earth

is reflected in patterns in the sky
and once we get that we *are* the dance
we can stretch our wings and fly:
> to attune to the seasons, moon and planets
> IS to find the way home –
> is the way out of delusion, disconnection, disaffection –
> it's time for humanity to renew the pact with life Herself

love and spirit connect us all
through prayer and compassion
we answer the call, build webs of love, cones of power
> invoking the return of Her magicians
> bringing humanity back to the Way
> in these dark 21st century days

The truth is within and it's out there too
Christian gnostics and heretics, Kabbalists and Sufi mystics
have long taught the way
Buddhist and Hindu sages were bringing the light of non-
duality to the west since the 19th century

> but the last thing the desire-driven, power-hungry west wanted
> to hear
> was that the ego was controlling the show and out of control –

our own European earth wisdom so long suppressed
we'd long forgotten our intrinsic belonging –
> yet now as Mother Earth shakes and and fear stalks the world,
> soon everyone on the planet may scream out to be whole
> the planet is in crisis, is humanity facing the end,
> or is everybody due **an Accelerated Discovery of Self.**

WHEN THE GODDESS RETURNS
people will fall to their knees
begging forgiveness for all our destructive deeds.

Humanity forgot how to love the Earth as Mother
forgot how to treat all living things as sister and brother.

> We take our Mother's blood in the form of oil
> we pollute and abuse her air, waters and soil
> not knowing we're her children
> intimately connected to her rhythms
> we continue to struggle, fight, create more schisms.

The Sun rises every day illuminating Who We Are
the Moon guides us along the way
the Stars tell us we will go far
when we rediscover how to pray
how our thoughts and intentions create our life experiences
that we are all one interconnected being.

The men of war killed Her priestesses and queer priests
shut down her temples, destroyed her groves and their holy
trees
until the populace no longer even believe
in the presence of Spirit, of the other planes
labelling those who communicate with them deluded or insane.

> Through the Goddess
> we know our ONENESS
> we feel our ancestors
> and nature's sprites.
> Through her rhythms
> we repair our souls.

By attuning to the sun and moon cycles
we can escape the delusion and confusion
of a society built on separation
and give birth to our healing nation.

The people of the Goddess are coming:
We're remembering that we lived before.
We're remembering a time before war
when sexuality was sacred
and all forms of love were honoured.

**We have to die to who we thought we were
to become who we've always been.**

*"A society that could heal the dismembered world would
recognise the inherent value of each person and of the plant,
animal and elemental life that makes us the earth's living body;
it would offer real protection, encourage free expression, and
re-establish an ecological balance to be biologically and
economically sustainable. Its underlying metaphor would be
mystery, the sense of wonder at all that is beyond us and
around us, at the forces that sustain our lives and the intricate
complexity and beauty of their dance."*

STARHAWK

PART 4

Departing

"And as to you death, and you bitter hug of mortality.. it is idle to try to alarm me......
And as to you corpse, i think you are good manure, but that does not offend me.....
And as to you life, i reckon you are the leavings of many deaths,
No doubt i have died myself ten thousand times before.
I hear you whispering there O stars of heaven....."

WALT WHITMAN

The Soul decides when it's time to go

the Body knows and it lets it show
We can resist, we can assist
Dying is inevitable but it's not the end
As the portals open
We can see, we can listen
Between the Worlds
To the Ancestors' songs
We might speak of what we see and hear
This will help release the fear
From all those at our side
We might remember why we came here
See the many gifts of being queer
Understand our connection to the invisible worlds
And bring through the blessings, the love unfurled

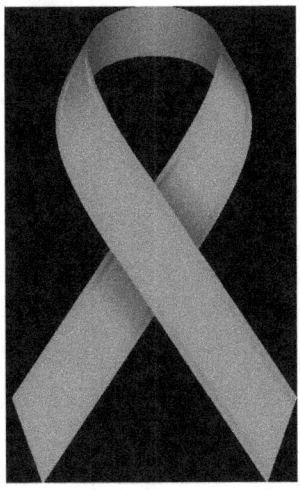

"Gayness is the coming together of certain strands of humanness. This particular arrangement, particular frequency, resonates well with certain functions in the human community. It is a nurturing frequency, a strong and caring one, that expresses itself in every possible way, yet excels at certain ones. To make art, to dance, to make beauty of body, food, home, all of these can be gifts of this energy. But working with those who are dying, working with death, is one of the skills that have been forgotten, not only by your community, but by the world itself. And many have died without the comforting hand of son, cousin, friend. But time brings all powers back to themselves. Time makes you remember this..."

From **Two Flutes Playing** by ANDREW RAMER

If we open ourselves to the flow of spirit through life and feel the existence of eternity within our own being, it gets easier to drop the fear of death. Then we really can become more alive, in the moment, open to what the universe offers us. We can drop the emotional loads we carry and forgive ourselves and others for the mistakes we have made due to fear or ignorance. We can literally enter into a new life, reborn to be miracle workers and help humanity stop fighting over beliefs and in time to take care of our ailing planet.

To get to know SPIRIT, focus on that, not on myths designed to scare the populace into obedience, and we can move on from the age of patriarchal control via religion and the sword, from the confusion and disrespect for life and the planet that has spread around the world, and re-enter the universal dance:

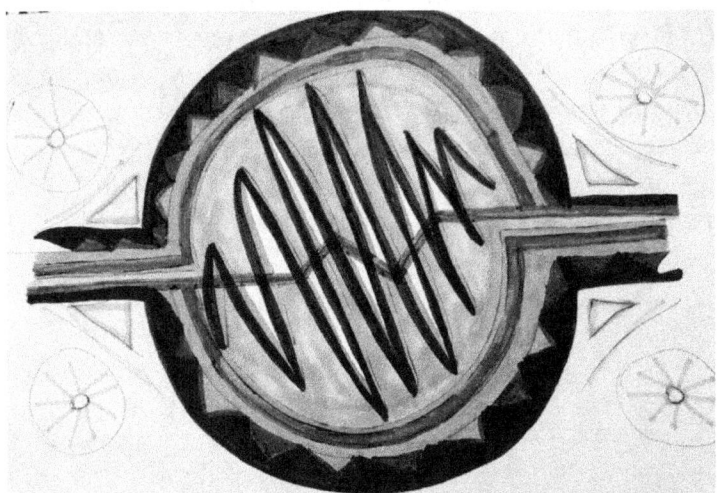

This was a lesson HIV and AIDS came into manifestation to teach us.

"Life does not begin at birth or end at death. Life extends beyond body and time, into and out of a spaciousness like the most powerful of dreams. Words alone cannot describe it. Perhaps 3-D film might one day do it, reveal the fluid vastness that life is. But one aspect of life is creating a body to focus yourself in. To do this is holy, to do this is a gift. You live in many bodies, as a painter paints many canvasses. Death is not the destruction of the artist. Death is the beginning of another phase in your timeless creativity...

"You as soul create many bodies to express yourself through, in different times, in different places, as female and male, as straight and gay. You are born many times and you die many times. Death is that part of the soul's process of recreating itself. The work of gay midwives to the dying is not easy. But you can tap into the place where you have done it before. You can tap into your guides, you can tap into the source of love, which permeates the universe. Love binds all together. No one is separate from love, from spirit. And death is not a separation. It is only a change in frequency."

From **Two Flutes Playing** by ANDREW RAMER

WHAT AIDS TAUGHT ME

When we are at peace about death we become more fully alive. Fear of dying blocks our spirit. It's a fear worth mastering, because death is all around us, always happening, and life is so rich, so full of amazement when we are open enough to see and feel it.

If we see death as a portal to the next stage of the journey we can take the chance and befriend it. When someone we love dies we can reach out to them through our hearts, and feel them reaching back. Through this we reconnect the worlds, we hasten the awakening, we find peace.

And the only way peace will prevail on planet earth is through each of us finding peace within ourselves.

Disease, War, Crime, Crisis, Climate Catastrophe

the 21st century world does not seem a happy place:
Chaos, Confusion, Corruption, Calamity
things looking rough for the human race.

But there's one missing element
one missing truth
that the world denies and won't see:
the one thing underlying all our crises
is our separation from eternity -
OUR LACK OF EXPERIENCE OF UNITY

All illness and abuse arise from the split
between humanity and the **LOVEFORCE** that created it:
this is not about religion, not even about god
this is about us discovering what's been going on all along.

My discovery came through facing death
opening my heart and mind to see
the presence of creation around and within me
this disease we call HIV
took me to the core of the matter
for **HIV is the middle name of SHIVA**

**sHIVa INVITES US TO RETHINK DEATH
TO OPEN TO KNOW OUR ETERNAL SOULS
A REVOLUTION IN HOW WE UNDERSTAND
LIFE ON EARTH -
THE ULTIMATE, ESSENTIAL, URGENT GOAL**

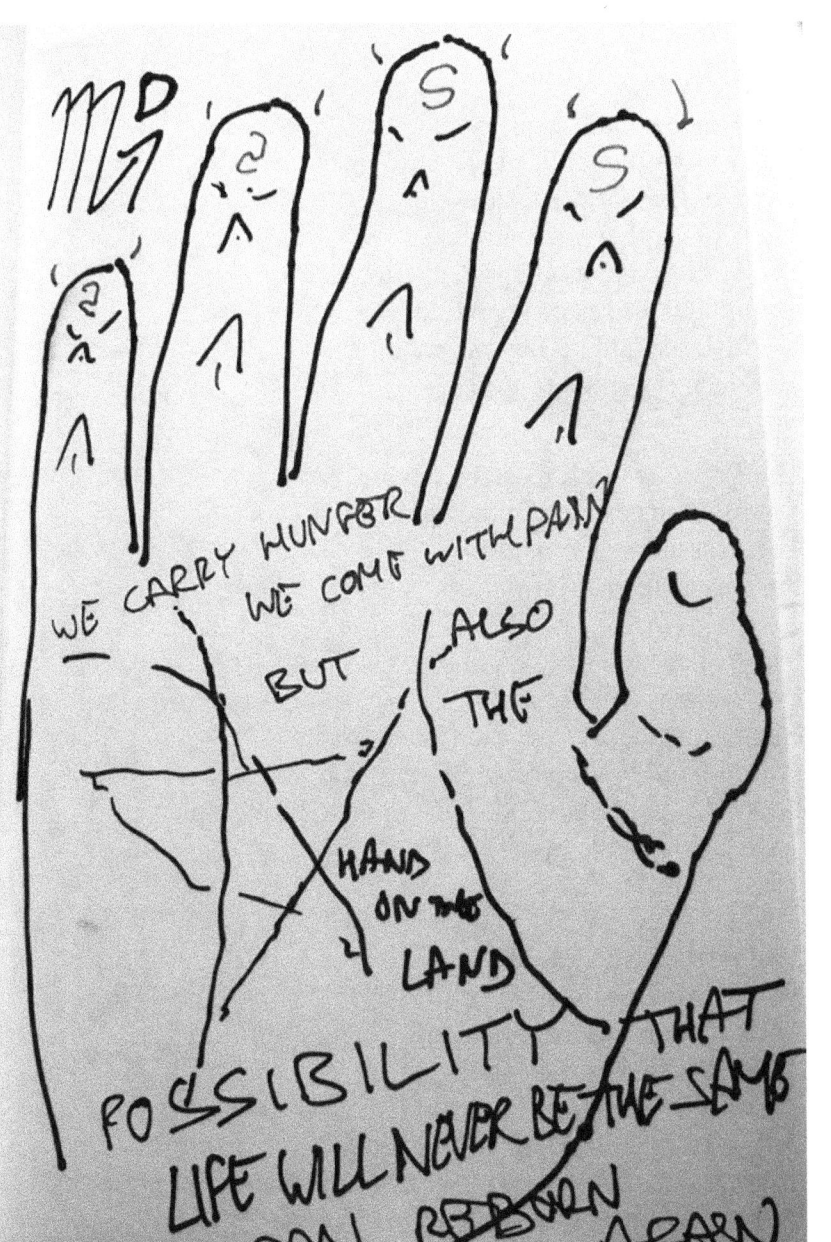

The Voices

The Voices that are angry
The Voices that are sad
The Voices that are jealous
The Voices that are mad
The Voices that are happy, excited, loving, kind
The many Voices of the Mind:
We observe and go beyond them
The deepest Voice to find.

The Wounds written on the Body
The Wounds carried in the Heart
The Pressures of Existence
Push us to Know our part.

Our Values and our Actions
Decree Who We Become
Our Friends and Lovers are our Mirrors
Reminding Us We are All One.
Beyond Illusion beyond Pain we Heal in the Spirit zone
The Caress of the Spirit Holy
The Divine Mother coming Home.

The Body is the gateway
The Mind a ladder to climb
The Heart is the seat of Soul
Spirit Unified is the Goal.
Mystics throughout time have prepared the Way
Our task in the 21st Century -
to Wake up the World, reveal a new way to Pray
Bring Ancient Light to Modern Times
Begin the Aquarian Day.

Stepping out of the Shadows

we reclaim our roles
step away from delusion
to clear out the confusion
uniting genders
uniting souls
the liberation of humankind
is the goal.

Female, male
between and beyond
queer, straight, homo, bi
we sing many songs
yet the core is the same
and awakening is the game
the Self is coming home
In radiant sunshine
and lunar reflections
Aquarian starlight
the divine perfection

when the goddess comes
it'll all make sense
our power was hidden
our power is immense
unlocking the gates to the multiverse
can only happen when
we are ready to serve.

The Spirit longs to reunite with the Living
Hear the Songs of All Souls as the Rainbow age rises,
all over the world people are remembering
we came here to heal this world and be whole.

The Spirit longs to reunite with the Living
Shamans everywhere across planet Earth are at their Gates.
Preparing for a decade of shifts so amazing -
To walk the healing path is to walk in Grace.

Shokti MMIX

www.ingramcontent.com/pod-product-compliance
Lightning Source LLC
Chambersburg PA
CBHW070304290526
45791CB00003B/1083